The Niagara River

The Niagara River

Melissa Whitcraft

Franklin Watts
A Division of Grolier Publishing
New York • London • Hong Kong • Sydney
Danbury, Connecticut

This one's for Jannie, Paul, and "the boys."

Note to readers: Definitions for words in **bold** can be found in the Glossary at the back of this book.

Photographs ©: AP/Wide World Photos: 40, 44, 48; Corbis-Bettmann: 23 (Lester V. Bergman), 19 top (Michael Freeman), 36, 43, (UPI), 8 (M.H. Zahner), 30; Liaison Agency, Inc.: 2 (Armen Kachaturian), 38, 49 (Andrew Klapatiuk); New England Stock Photo: 22 (Roger Bickel), cover, 16 top, 19 bottom (Jim Schwabel); North Wind Picture Archives: 14, 16 bottom; Stock Montage, Inc.: 18, 51; Visuals Unlimited: 46 (Gary Carter), 5 right, 20, (Nada Pecnik), 24, 28 (Rob & Ann Simpson), 12 (John Sohlden); Wolfgang Käehler: 5 left, 6, 11, 26, 27, 32, 34.

(p. 10) Map by Bob Italiano.

The photograph on the cover shows the Horseshoe Falls. The photograph opposite the title page shows Niagara Falls.

Visit Franklin Watts on the Internet at:
http://publishing.grolier.com

Library of Congress Cataloging-in-Publication Data

Whitcraft, Melissa
    The Niagara River / by Melissa Whitcraft
        p.   cm.— (Watts library)
    Includes bibliographical references and index.
    ISBN 0-531-11903-3 (lib. bdg.)   0-531-13987-5 (pbk.)
        1. Niagara River Valley (N.Y. and Ont.)—History—Juvenile literature. 2. Niagara River Valley (N.Y. and Ont.)—Description and travel—Juvenile literature. 3. Niagara River (N.Y. and Ont.)—History—Juvenile literature. 4. Niagara River (N.Y. and Ont.)—Description and travel—Juvenile literature. [1. Niagara River (N.Y. and Ont.) 2. Niagara River Valley (N.Y. and Ont.)] I. Title. II. Series.
F127 .N6 W56 2001
971.3'38—dc21   00-039928

Contents

People from around the world visit the Niagara Falls each year.

Chapter One

The Daring Niagara

The Niagara River is known for its most famous landmark—the Niagara Falls. While some visitors come to the falls to see its beauty, others have been lured by the possibility of adventure. Trying to go over the falls can be a dangerous trip, as one man described it:

"You drop the barrel into the water about 200 yards upstream. It's pretty quiet on the float down. You hear only a little bit of water outside. . . . All of a sudden,

your heart is in your stomach and you're falling straight down. It's roaring loud inside the barrel. . . I went down headfirst and landed between two big rocks."

This is how Steve Trotter described his plunge over Niagara Falls in 1985. The experience cost him $5,500 in fines. Going over the falls in a barrel, even if it is a fancy modern contraption complete with walkie-talkies, has been illegal in Canada and the United States for more than fifty years. Ever since October 24, 1901, however, when Annie Edson Taylor was the first, Niagara daredevils have challenged death to conquer the falls. Some, like Taylor and Trotter, lived to talk about it. Others died trying.

Annie Edson Taylor crosses the river after surviving the trip over the falls.

A Small, Mighty River

Issuing out of Lake Erie at Buffalo, New York, the Niagara flows north for only 35 miles (56.3 kilometers) before emptying into Lake Ontario. However, the small river serves as an international border. With the province of Ontario to its west and the state of New York to the east, it forms a fraction of the 5,335-mile (8,586-km) long border between Canada and the United States.

The Niagara splits into two channels approximately 3 miles (5 km) from its source to go around Grand Island. Here, the current flows at a calm 5 miles (8 km) an hour. At the rapids, which are 3 miles (5 km) south of the falls, the water races at 41 miles (68 km) an hour.

At the falls, the river splits again around Goat Island and the smaller Luna Island, creating the river's two **cataracts**. The American Falls are 182 feet (55 meters) high and have an

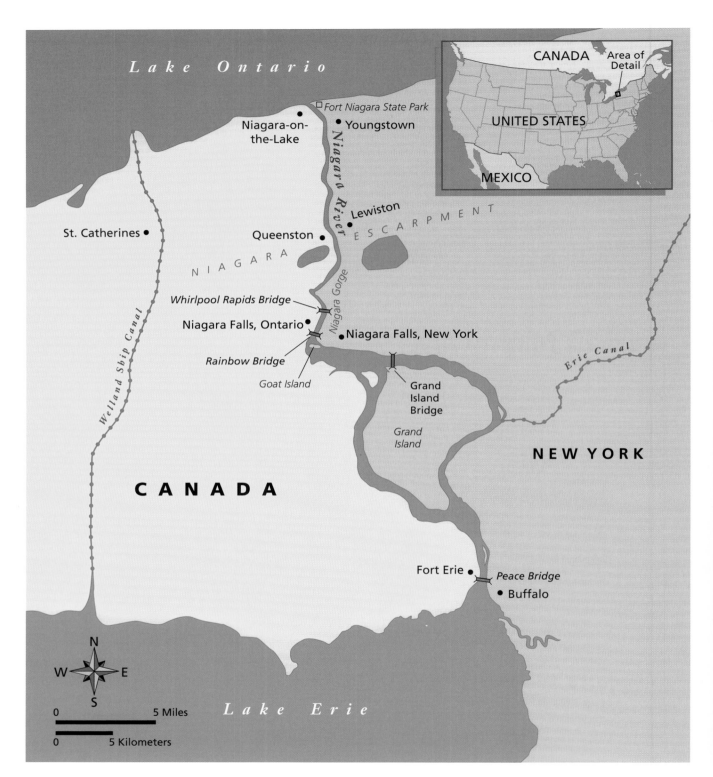

almost straight **crestline** of 1,075 feet (328 meters) across. The Canadian Horseshoe Falls are 176 feet (54 m) high and 2,100 feet (640 m) across. Even though the American Falls are higher, the Canadian Falls carry approximately nine times the water because of their longer, "horseshoe" arch.

This photo shows the Niagara River near Lake Ontario.

When the Niagara River pours over the falls, its volume equals 6 million cubic feet (168,000 cubic meters) of water per minute. In less scientific terms, try to imagine one million bathtubs full of water going over the falls every second. Once past the falls, the swift current curves through the Niagara **Gorge** and the Whirlpool Rapids before emptying into Lake Ontario. The trip is not long. Yet, the tiny Niagara which some call a **strait**, not a river, is mightier than it appears.

Where does its power come from? In part, it comes from the river's **topography**. The Niagara is the main drainage outlet for the upper Great Lakes. These waters pour out of Lake Erie and are funneled down the Niagara into Lake Ontario. In addition, at its source, the Niagara is 569 feet (173 m) above sea level. When it reaches its mouth, the river is only 246 feet (75 m) above sea level. This steep drop of 323 feet (98 m) in 35 miles (56.3 km), coupled with the river's constant water flow, is what gives the Niagara its extraordinary power.

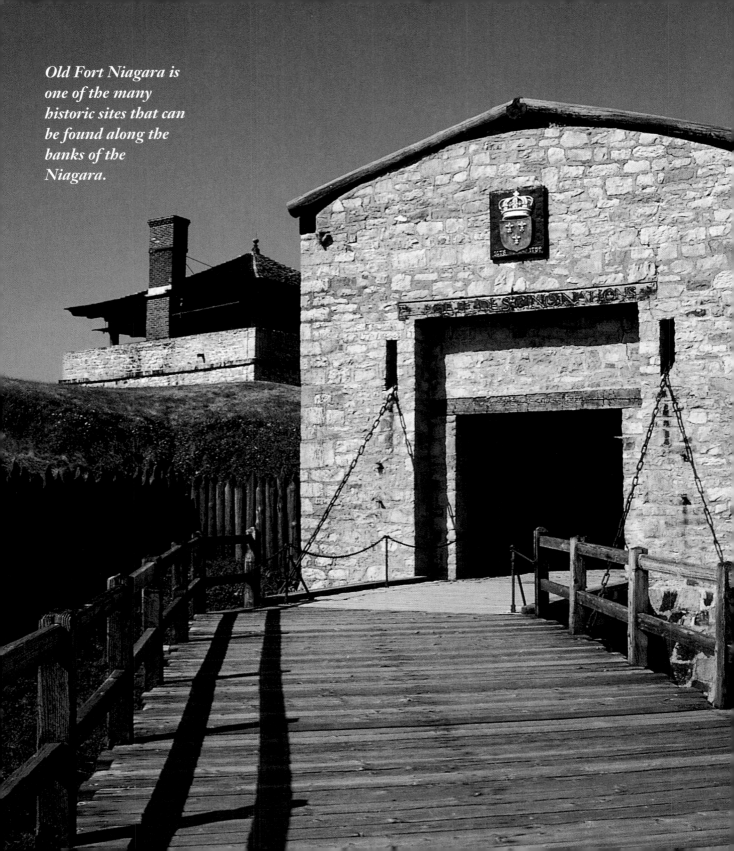

Old Fort Niagara is one of the many historic sites that can be found along the banks of the Niagara.

Chapter Two

The Historic Niagara

Along with the towns, cities, hydroelectric plants, factories, and parks that line the banks of the Niagara are the historic monuments, plaques, museums, and houses that speak to an earlier time. For, as modern as the Niagara region is, it is also an area rich in history. Reconstructed forts from the 1700s guard the river's mouth and source. The Mac-Farland House, a small museum along the west bank, stands as the only remaining pre-1812 house in the region. All others were destroyed in the War of 1812. In addition, traveling south from Niagara-on-Lake, numerous plaques mark sites where battles took place, and orchards planted by British settlers still produce fruit for roadside farm stands.

The First People

The Mound Builders were the indigenous people who originally settled the lands around the Niagara. They were a sophisticated trading society that migrated north from the Ohio Valley in approximately 1000 B.C. By the 1400s, various tribes were in the area. One particular group, called the

This 1771 map shows where the six nations lived in the Niagara area.

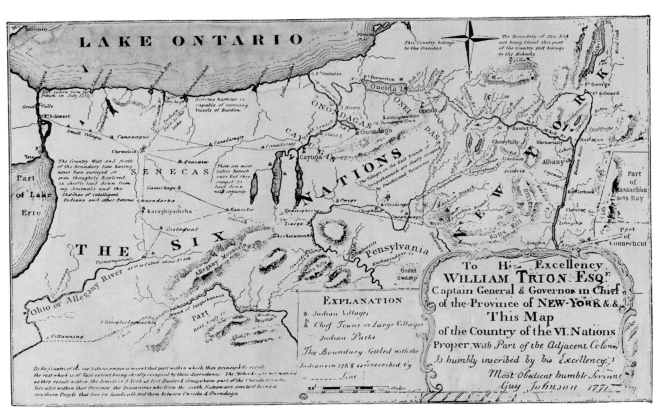

Neutrals by some, was known as a peaceful tribe who did not take sides between the warring Huron and Iroquois. It is their word, *onghiara*, which gives us, *Niagara*. *Onghiara* means "throat" or "strait" and refers to the river's location between Lake Erie and Lake Ontario.

By the 1650s, the Iroquois League of Five Nations was firmly established on the Niagara. Formed around 1570, the League consisted of five tribes, all of whom shared similar cultures and language. They were the Mohawk, Seneca, Cayuga, Onondaga, and Oneida. When the British in North Carolina defeated the Tuscarora in 1713, that tribe moved north to the Niagara region. Around 1722, they too joined the Iroquois, making it the League of Six Nations.

The Arrival of Europeans

Ever since the Frenchman, Jacques Cartier, first came to the St. Lawrence River in 1534, Europeans had probably heard stories about the Niagara with its spectacular falls. The first to have seen them is thought to be **friar** Louis Hennepin. Hennepin was a member of the advance party for the explorer, René-Robert Cavelier, Sieur de La Salle. La Salle later claimed the territory for France and built a fur trading station on the east bank of the Niagara's mouth. The settlement burnt down but was rebuilt later as Fort Niagara.

If the French were the first Europeans to build at the mouth of the Niagara, they were not the only Europeans who wanted to control the river. The British also wanted a

Fort Niagara

Built in 1726, Fort Niagara was controlled at various times by the French, the British, Canadian colonists, and American revolutionaries. Across the river from Niagara-on-the-Lake, the fort is now a living museum outside Youngstown, New York.

Iroquois warriors helped the British fight the French in the French and Indian War.

stronghold along its banks. Eventually, the desire to control all of North America led to the French and Indian War.

The war lasted from 1754 to 1763 with both sides enlisting the help of American Indian tribes. The Algonquians fought with the French, the Iroquois with the British. Each tribe hoped that the side it had chosen would respect its rights when the fighting was over.

The Iroquois expected the British to honor their promise to never settle or hunt along the Niagara. When the war ended, however, and the French lost all their holdings, the British went wherever they wanted. Often, they were seen traveling on the Iroquois's steep 9-mile (14.4-km) **portage** around Niagara Falls.

In retaliation, several hundred Senecas, who had not been allies of the British, ambushed a wagon train and its military escort. Despite help from Fort Niagara, the

16

wagons were thrown over the Niagara Gorge at a point called Devil's Hole. At least one hundred people were killed. Sir William Johnson, who commanded Fort Niagara, was so outraged that he demanded the Indians give up the portage. To insure British control of the route, he built stockades along the trail and constructed Fort Erie at the Niagara's source.

The British continued to control both sides of the Niagara until after the American Revolution. At the time, Niagara's east bank went to the United States. Loyalists, those British settlers who chose to remain under British rule, fled and resettled on the Niagara's west bank.

Niagara-on-the-Lake

Many loyalists ended up in Niagara-on-the-Lake, which was a stronghold for the British because of its location. Ships that came through the St. Lawrence and across Lake Ontario unloaded here because the river was impassable. From this point on, all goods and passengers bound for the upper Great Lakes had to go overland.

Lake Ontario

Lake Ontario, the fourteenth largest lake in the world, is the smallest of North America's five Great Lakes. The lake is 193 miles (311 km) long and 53 miles (85 km) wide and flows from the mouth of the Niagara to the St. Lawrence Seaway. The St. Lawrence Seaway connects the Great Lakes to the Atlantic Ocean. *Ontario* comes from an Iroquois word meaning either "beautiful lake" or "rocks standing near water."

A soldier's wife helps to defend Fort Niagara during the War of 1812.

The War of 1812 threatened the British rule on the Niagara. The fighting started because the United States wanted to stop the British from taking American sailors off American ships to become soldiers for Britain in their war against France. Settlements all along the Niagara were drawn into the conflict because the Americans believed that if they defeated the Canadian colonists, they would defeat England. Given its importance as a port, Niagara-on-the-Lake was particularly vulnerable. When the Americans captured the town, they burned it to the ground. At the end of the war, all lands that had been taken were returned to the country that originally controlled them.

Niagara-on-the-Lake flourished again until the 1830s when the Welland Ship Canal was built 8.5 miles (13.6 km) north in St. Catherines. Connecting Lake Ontario to Lake

Erie, the canal made it possible for ships to bypass the area. As a result, Niagara-on-the-Lake became a ghost town.

In recent years, the town has come back to life, in part because of its ghosts. Niagara-on-the-Lake now bustles with life because it has become a popular spot for tourists. Visitors enjoy the town's shade-speckled side streets, antique shops and mid-1800s houses. There are clapboard inns built in the 1830s, large Victorian hotels, and old cemeteries. The local historical society, founded in 1895, has a collection of more than twenty thousand artifacts. The past surrounds you everywhere in this town that has become the keeper of the river's rich history.

The Welland Ship Canal

The Welland Ship Canal is 27 miles (43.5 km) long. To compensate for the difference in sea level between Lake Ontario and Lake Erie, the canal is equipped with eight **canal locks** that allow ships to pass up and down from one lake to the other.

The Prince of Wales Hotel is one of the historic places in Niagara-on-the-Lake.

The Whirlpool Rapids are part of the Niagara River Gorge.

Chapter Three

The Geological Niagara

Upriver from Niagara-on-the-Lake, past the massive Sir Adam Beck–Niagara twin hydroelectric power plants and a countryside filled with roadside vegetable stands, the river winds through a steep rocky gorge. The cliffs might not rival the majesty of the falls, but they are part of what makes the Niagara such a geological wonderland.

21

Dangerous Whirlpool

Throughout the 1800s, people tried to cross the Whirlpool Rapids. Similar to those who went over the falls, some people survived, but others didn't. In the 1970s, tour groups attempted to take people across in white water rafts, but the ride too dangerous. Rafts tipped over and people drowned. However, people have been crossing safely by aerial cable car for nearly one hundred years.

At the Whirlpool Rapids section of the Gorge, the Niagara shoots down its main channel before veering off into a high circular hollow that bulges out to the left. Inside this hollow, or pocket, the water whirls in a counter clockwise direction. If the water level is high, the circular flow is so powerful it forces incoming water under the swirling current. Called a reversal phenomenon, the process creates a whirlpool, or vortex, that is 125 feet (38 m) deep.

As intriguing as the whirlpool is, it is the stratified layers of rock that make up the Niagara Gorge that are endlessly fascinating to geologists. Ancient sea **fossils** found in these layers tell scientists that long before the Niagara was a river, approximately 450 million years ago, most of central North America was under an immense shallow sea. The stratification of the soil at the gorge represents the debris that settled on the bottom of this sea over thousands of years.

Niagara Fossils

Two examples of fossils found in the Niagara Gorge are trilobites and sea lilies. Most trilobites were small bottom-feeding crustaceans. They became extinct more than 200 million years ago. Spidery sea lilies can still be found in the Atlantic Ocean and tropical seas. They begin life on the sea bottom. Some stay rooted there, but others leave their roots to become floating "feather stars."

The Niagara Escarpment

These layers of limestone form part of the Niagara Escarpment.

Once the sea dried up, the Niagara region became a flat plain. Over millions of years, as the earth's crust moved, the plain shifted. This shift created an enormous ridge, broken in places, that has a steep cliff on one side and a long gentle slope on the other. Called an escarpment, this ridge stretches 1,000 miles (1,609 km) from Watertown, New York, to Manitoulin Island, Ontario. Because the ridge is made of basaltic rock—dark gray-to-black colored rock formed by volcanic activity—that resists **erosion**, it is higher than the surrounding land. As a result, the escarpment creates a landform that resembles a huge saucer-shaped basin.

The Niagara Escarpment is a 450-mile (725-km) section of the entire ridge. While Niagara Falls is the most famous part, the escarpment is filled with more than one hundred important geological sites. Viewed as one of the world's greatest natural wonders, it was named a

24

World Biosphere Reserve by the United Nations Educational, Scientific and Cultural Organization (UNESCO) in 1990. As part of the biosphere reserve program, scientists study and monitor the area's environment.

The Ice Age

The question remains as to how the Niagara plain with its escarpment changed to become the Niagara River. To solve this mystery, geologists look back about 1.6 million years ago. During this period, which is sometimes called the Ice Age, glaciers inched down over much of North America and Europe.

When the ice melted and the glaciers pulled back, both the Great Lakes and the Niagara River were formed. The river was shaped when the last glacier, called the Laurentide Ice Sheet, retreated from the region approximately 12,000 years ago. When the runoff from the melting ice ran out of ancient Lake Erie into what is now Lake Ontario, its route became the Niagara River.

No Overnight Wonder

The ice age began slowly, very slowly, when the Earth's temperature began to change, dropping only a few degrees a season. Winters got longer, springs shorter, until the snows of one winter lasted all year long. The accumulating snow compressed into heavy layers of ice. These massive ice sheets, some of which were over 2 miles (3.2 km) thick, covered almost everything in their path and carved huge depressions in the land.

Shrinking Gorge, Moving Falls

The water that flows from the upper Great Lakes continues to erode both the Niagara Gorge and the escarpment. Sections of the gorge have slid into the river and, since they were formed, the Canadian Falls have moved back 7 miles (11 km) from the original Escarpment brow. Originally, they were closer to Queenston, Ontario. On the other hand, the American Falls, because they carry only 10 percent of the river's flow, have moved very little.

The Canadian Falls, also called the Horseshoe Falls, are eroding faster than the American Falls.

To find out why the falls move, geologists turned again to ancient geological history. When a sea covered the region millions of years ago, the soil layers formed by the shells and coral reefs turned into a hard limestone rock called dolomite. The top layer of the Niagara Escarpment is dolomite.

When water pours over the escarpment and crashes into the riverbed below, the turbulence weakens the shale and sandstone layers under the escarpment's dolomite cap. As these softer layers disintegrate, the heavy dolomite layer loses its support. Eventually a section breaks off creating a V-shaped ridge in the crestline. Over time the ridge smoothes out, and the erosive process begins again.

Geologists know how far the falls have moved by studying the river's plunge pools. Plunge pools, or plunge basins, are pools of water that form directly under the crestline of the falls. Niagara's old plunge pools still exist further downstream. They provide an accurate chart for scientists to measure the falls progress back towards Lake Erie. To estimate how long the falls were at a given place, scientists measure the depth of the plunge pool. The deeper the pool, the longer the falls were above it.

The Erosion Rate

Until recently the erosion rate of the falls was approximately 3 feet (90 centimeters) a year. By diverting the Niagara's flow into hydroelectric plants, the Americans and Canadians have slowed the erosion down to less than 1 foot (30 cm) a year.

People have relied on the Niagara as source of power since the mid-1700s.

Chapter Four

The Powerful Niagara

At the head of the Niagara Gorge, Niagara Falls towers over the river below. While many have marveled at its beauty, others have seen the falls as a source of endless energy. People have been looking for ways to tap into this energy as early as 1757 when Daniel Joncaire built a water-powered sawmill. But, it took the invention of **hydroelectricity**—using the river's water to create electricity—before the Niagara's full energy potential was realized.

Harnessing the River

To oversee how electric companies used the Niagara, the International Niagara Commission was formed at the end of the 1800s. The commission sought the expertise of four European scientists who, in turn, asked many companies to compete for the chance to build the first power plants at the Niagara. The idea of generating huge amounts of electricity had never been considered before. All concerned wanted to make sure the right decisions were made.

One of the more famous scientists involved with the Commission was Nikola Tesla, a Croatian-American. Tesla worked for the American manufacturer, George Westing-house. Tesla discovered how to create electricity by using a

Nikola Tesla works in his laboratory.

rotating magnetic field that produced two alternating currents. Unlike Thomas Edison's direct current (DC), Tesla's alternating current (AC) electricity made it possible for high voltages of electrical current to be sent safely through wires over hundreds of miles. As a result, his AC electricity system was the best system to use and Westinghouse received the contract to build the first two plants on the Niagara. Today, Tesla's AC current is the basis for almost all electrical current in the world.

The first large-scale hydroelectric facility, the Edward Dean Adams Power Plant, began operating on the American side of the river in 1896. The plant operated until June 7, 1956, when it was destroyed in a rock slide. The slide pushed the plant down into the Niagara Gorge.

On the Canadian side, the Ontario Power Company built a hydroelectric **generator** at the foot of Horseshoe Falls in 1905. In 1922, Sir Adam Beck, the first chairman of Ontario

Early Entrepreneurs

Augustus Porter and his brother, Peter, were two of the first businessmen who saw the potential in the Niagara. In 1805, they bought riverfront land from the state of New York and built a water-powered gristmill on one site. They offered other sites for sale hoping to bring more business to the river, but no one followed their lead. Their vision of an industrial Niagara was ahead of its time. In 1815, recognizing the beauty of the area as well, Augustus Porter bought Goat Island to keep as a nature preserve. Today, it is still a natural park with no commercial development.

Sir Adam Beck Generating Station in Ontario, Canada.

Hydro, built Niagara Generating Station Number One outside Queenston. It was Beck's dream to offer inexpensive electrical power to all who wanted it.

How Water Becomes Power

Today we have electricity at the flip of a switch. Without thinking, we use electricity—turning on lights, playing music on our CD players, and watching television. But how does that electrical energy get from its source to the switch?

At Niagara Generating Station Number One, river water from above Niagara Falls is diverted into underground gathering tubes that are 46 feet (14 m) in diameter. These tubes carry the water to a reservoir called a forebay. From the forebay, the water flows down a shute, or penstock, to the turbines. The force of the water spins the turbine's paddle wheel. At this point, the water is released back into the river through an exit pipe called the tailrace.

At the same time, the rotating paddle wheel turns the turbine shaft, which rotates the generator shaft. The generator shaft then spins magnets that are inside wire coils. The AC electricity created by this action travels through wires from the generator to a transformer station.

From the transformer station, transmission lines take the electricity to distribution stations. There, the electricity, again moving through wires, is sent to a substation transformer before it is routed into particular neighborhoods. To reduce the power to a safe voltage, the electricity passes into a smaller pole transformer before it finally enters individual buildings. When it does, there is electricity, all at the flip of a switch!

The Niagara Diversion Treaty

Realizing the effect their hydroelectric plants would have on the river, Canada and the United States signed the Niagara Diversion Treaty in 1950. The agreement stated that neither country could divert the Niagara's water to its power plants at the expense of the falls. No one wanted to turn its mighty wall of water into a tiny trickle.

Once the treaty was signed, both countries built immense hydroelectric plants on both sides of the river. Canada added to the first Beck plant by building a second station. It was completed in 1958. Today, the two Beck plants can produce 1.8 million **kilowatt**-hours of electricity.

In the United States, the New York State Power Authority, headed by Robert Moses, built a similar structure at Lewiston. Completed in 1963 and known as the Robert Moses–Niagara Power Plant, the facility has a capacity to create 2.4 million kilowatt-hours.

The Robert Moses–Niagara Power Plant takes water from the Niagara to make energy.

The Blackout

While much of the electricity produced at the Niagara is used in Ontario and northern New York state, additional power is carried throughout the Northeast. The entire system is called the Northeast power grid or CANUSE, for Canadian United States Energy. For the most part, CANUSE has functioned without many serious glitches. There was one extraordinary night, however, when the unimaginable happened. Approximately 80,000 square miles (207,200 square kilometers) of North America went dark.

Known as the blackout, the problem started at 5:27 P.M. on November 9, 1965. A safety device no larger than a pay telephone at the Sir Adam Beck Generating Plant Number Two malfunctioned. As a result safety switches in station after station were tripped. Twenty minutes later the entire CANUSE system was down. More than 30 million people were left without electricity.

A commercial pilot flying 30,000 feet (9,150 m) over New York City looked out to see the entire metropolitan area disappear. Another pilot flying over Boston saw the same thing

Police lead people out of the subway system in New York City during the blackout.

happen there. No one knew what was going on. One young boy was terrified that he had caused the disaster because he hit a telephone pole with a stick the instant the lights went out.

The blackout started at rush hour, right when the roads and subways were most crowded. In Toronto, electric streetcars, filled with people, just stopped. In New York City, thousands of subway passengers were caught underground. Nearly 800,000 people were stranded on electric commuter trains. Firemen had to rescue people caught in skyscraper elevators, and five hundred flights were diverted from the darkened airports.

People living in the Niagara region only experienced a blackout for a short period of time. The area had so many substations that most of the electricity returned by 7:00 P.M. Other places weren't as lucky. In New York City, it took 14 hours to restore power.

Throughout the Northeast people responded well. Volunteers directed traffic. Strangers calmed each other. Neighbors helped neighbors. Once everyone knew the problem was nothing more than a power failure, there was an almost festive atmosphere as everyone worked together during the crisis.

The electricity from power plants on the Niagara enabled businesses to thrive on its banks.

Chapter Five

The Industrial Niagara

At the end of the 1800s, the character of the Niagara changed, especially on the American side of the river. Hydroelectricity would alter the face of the town of Niagara Falls, New York. Dreamers and businesspeople alike flocked to the river to build factories that ran on this amazing new source of energy. In the past, factories had depended on coal, which was dirty and messy. Now electricity provided people with a new source of clean and easily renewable power.

Early Dreamers

One of the first visionaries to come to Niagara Falls, New York, was William T. Love. In 1893, he planned to build a spectacular manufacturing city with a 7-mile (11.2-km) long canal, which would channel water from the river to the city's hydroelectric plant. Before he ran out of money, Love did build a small portion of this canal.

King Camp Gillette's plans for a Niagara Falls community were even grander than Love's. His city next to the river would contain the entire population of the United States. His vision was never realized, and today Gillette is better known for his 1903 invention, the Gillette Safety Razor.

Love and Gillette failed to realize their dreams, but Henry D. Perky succeeded with his. In 1901, he opened his "Temple of Cleanliness" which he described as the "cleanest, finest, most hygienic factory in the world." Here, he produced his health cereal, Shredded Wheat, which is still on the market today.

The Rise of Factories

Charles Martin Hall moved to Niagara Falls in 1893. Hall had discovered how to make aluminum—a strong, light metal that didn't tarnish. The process called for vast amounts of electric energy. The Niagara Falls Power Company agreed to supply Hall's factory with all the electricity it needed. Today, Hall's company, the Aluminum Company of America, ALCOA, is the world's number one manufacturer of aluminum.

By 1909, there were twenty-two manufacturing businesses in the area lured by the promise of cheap hydroelectric power. Some like Union Carbide, American Cyanamide, Occidental Petroleum, and Auto-Lite Battery became very well known. These companies produced different products, such as bleaches and batteries, but they did have one thing in common. All of the companies depended on the electrical power created by the Niagara.

After World War II, Niagara Falls experienced another burst of industrial development when chemical companies

Life on the Other Side

In contrast to the industrial development of the New York side of the falls, Niagara Falls, Ontario, became a popular tourist spot with an amusement park and daredevil exhibits.

moved into the area. Soon factories were manufacturing medicines, plastics, pesticides, weed killers, dyes, fabrics, and preservatives. Producing these goods created chemical waste. During this time, most scientists did not know how dangerous the chemical waste could be—they thought it was harmless. Companies simply buried their waste materials in the soil or dumped it in the river.

We now know, however, that these wastes can be extremely dangerous. Once waste has seeped into the soil or water, it can survive for years. Scientists believe that these wastes can harm animals and humans.

Love Canal Revisited

In 1947, the Hooker Corporation bought the 1-mile (1.6-km) long canal that Love built. The company filled the canal with thousands of 55-gallon (209-liter) metal barrels. The barrels, containing 20,000 tons (20,320 metric tons) of chemical waste, were then covered with clay and dirt.

Lois Gibbs

Lois Gibbs lived with her family in Love Canal. With no previous experience, she became an advocate for the community when she learned about the chemical contamination. As president of the Love Canal Homeowners Association, she fought to get the government to pay to relocate those families whose property was condemned. Today, she is the executive director for the National Citizen's Clearinghouse for Hazardous Waste in Falls Church, Virginia. This organization helps communities throughout the country deal with toxic dumpsites in their neighborhoods.

To house all the people who moved to Niagara Falls to take jobs in the chemical industries, builders constructed many new homes and created new neighborhoods. Love Canal became one of the new neighborhoods in town, built over the site where all the barrels had been buried. By the early 1960s, the buried chemicals started to make their way to the surface. Children played with **phosphorus** "firerocks" that burned their hands. Paint on houses turned black.

By 1975, chemical waste was bubbling up into people's basements, and the area had an unusual number of people who had cancer, disease, and birth defects compared to other places. Eventually the government declared the area too hazardous for people to live there. Nine hundred families were evacuated, and in 1980 President Carter gave the state of New York $15 million to compensate the displaced residents.

In January 1996, the Justice Department and the Environmental Protection Agency (EPA) declared that after a massive clean up, some

A child sits outside the Love Canal section of Niagara Falls.

43

A worker tries to clean up Love Canal.

parts of Love Canal were now fit for people to live there. There are still pockets of contamination, however, and legal battles continue. Occidental Petroleum, which is the parent company for the Hooker Corporation, paid millions of dollars to the Love Canal residents who had sued them. The company, in turn, is now suing the state of New York and the town of Niagara Falls to help finance the continuing clean up of the area.

There is still work to be done. Love Canal only opened the door to a larger problem—one that involves more than one site and one company. It will take years to clean the Niagara region of the toxins that have contaminated the soil, the river, and Lake Ontario. Nevertheless, progress is slowly being made. Industries no longer dump their chemical waste into the ground, nor do they discharge it into the river. Laws such as the 1989 New York State Hazardous Waste Reduction Act forbid it. There are also programs on both sides of the river that are committed to cleaning the Niagara up. Two of the most recent ones are the Canadian and the U.S. Niagara River Remedial Action Plans (RAP) and the Canadian/U.S. Niagara River Toxics Management Plan (NRTMP).

Adventurous people like Charles Blondin have crossed from the American side to the Canadian side of Niagara Falls.

Chapter Six

Bridging The Niagara

Ever since the Iroquois built their portage up the east side of the river, people have looked for ways to cross the Niagara. The daredevil, Jean Francois Gravelet, known as Charles Blondin, was one of the more inventive. On June 30, 1859, he walked across on a rope that stretched 1,100 feet (330 m) from the American side to the Canadian side. Balancing 150 feet (46 m) above the current, Blondin repeated this stunt in several different ways over the years—

John Augustus Roebling built many famous bridges, including the Brooklyn Bridge.

blindfolded, carrying a man on his back, and pushing a wheelbarrow.

In the mid-1800s, railroad travel brought an explosion of tourists to Niagara Falls. There was, however, no way to get the fifty thousand visitors a year across the river. Most did not want to take the small ferry that braved the turbulent current. The Niagara needed a railroad bridge. The American engineer Charles Ellett, Jr. was contracted to do the job. In 1848, his bridge—the first across the river—opened. But, because of friction over the project, it only carried horse and carriage trade.

John Augustus Roebling built the Niagara's first railway **suspension bridge**. Opening on March 18, 1855, it was also the world's first. It weighed 1,000 tons (1,016 metric tons) and was hung from huge iron cables. Roebling, the first engineer to build suspension bridges that didn't sway, invented the technique of twisting thin strands of steel together to strengthen the bridges. Each of the cables for this bridge was made from

The Niagara's First Toll Bridge

In 1817 Augustus Porter constructed the Niagara's first toll bridge to take visitors to his nature preserve on Goat Island.

Rebuilt in 1818, the bridge was 700 feet (213.4 m) long and came within 150 feet (45.7 m) of the crest of the American Falls.

3,640 separate wires spun together. Roebling is best known as the designer of New York's famous Brooklyn Bridge.

Today, five bridges span the Niagara River—the bridge from Lewiston, New York, to Queenston, Ontario; the Whirlpool Rapids Bridge; the Rainbow Bridge; the Grand Island Bridge; and the Peace Bridge. The Peace Bridge connects Buffalo, New York, and Fort Erie, Ontario, at the Niagara's source by Lake Erie. A vital link for passenger cars and international truck trade, the bridge is also a symbol of friendship between Canada and the United States. Built in 1927, it commemorates the peace that has existed between the two countries since the War of 1812.

The Rainbow Bridge connects Niagara Falls, New York, with Niagara Falls, Ontario.

Lake Erie

Lake Erie is the fourth largest of the Great Lakes. At 241 miles (388 km) long and 57 miles (92 km) wide, Erie is the shallowest of the lakes with an average depth of 62 feet (19 m).

Crossing to Freedom

Built by the British in 1764, Fort Erie is called "The Gateway to Canada." Fort Erie certainly was the gateway to freedom for the twelve thousand to sixty thousand escaped slaves who

The War of 1812

During the War of 1812, men of African descent living in Canada formed their own military unit. Begun by the black Loyalist, Richard Pierpont, but commanded by a white officer, the "Colored Corps" fought for the British, believing they would lose their freedom if the United States won the war.

fled the United States in the years before the Civil War. Settlements up and down the Canadian side of the Niagara became welcomed destinations for these freedom seekers.

Many former slaves settled in the lands around Fort Erie. Here, for the first time, they lived as free men and women. They worked in local lumber mills and shipyards. Some even became farmers who owned their own land.

Life was good for the escaped slaves in Canada, but some returned to the United States after the Civil War to be reunited with their families. The Canadian side of the Niagara, however, continued to play an important role in the history of African Americans.

The Niagara Movement

African-Americans had won their freedom, but most were still segregated from white society in 1905. William E. B. Du Bois, the first black to graduate from Harvard with a doctorate, organized a conference to consider the continuing issue of African-American rights. Deciding to meet in Buffalo, Du Bois and other African-American intellectuals arrived only to discover that all the hotels were segregated.

Crossing over into Fort Erie, the group registered in a Canadian hotel, where they wrote a Declaration of Principles. These principles were the foundation for a new organization called the Niagara Movement. The Niagara Movement declared that there must be an end to all class distinctions based on race and color. Acknowledging the dignity of labor, the movement also demanded that African-Americans be given the same educational opportunities as whites.

In 1909, Du Bois' organization joined with a white **liberal** political group to become the National Association for the Advancement of Colored People. The NAACP continues to be a champion for African-American rights.

The principles of the Niagara Movement are almost one hundred years old—not nearly as ancient as the river that shares its name, but hopefully as enduring. Likewise, the continuing friendship between the United States and Canada will ensure that the Niagara, this surprising river with its varied past and powerful majesty, will remain mighty for thousands of years to come.

This photo shows W.E.B. Du Bois and the other members of Niagara Movement.

Timeline

1000 B.C.	The Mound Builders settle in the lands around the Niagara River.
1570s	The Iroquois League of Five Nations is formed and includes the Mohawk, Seneca, Cayuga, Onondaga, and Oneida.
1650s	The Iroquois League of Five Nations establishes itself in the Niagara area.
circa 1722	The Tuscarora join the Iroquois, making it the Iroquois League of Six Nations.
1726	Fort Niagara is built.
1754–1763	The French and Indian War is fought and the British capture Fort Niagara.
1757	Daniel Joncaire uses the waters of the Niagara to power his sawmill.
1805	Augustus and Peter Porter buy land on the Niagara River and build a water-powered gristmill.
1812–1814	The United States fights Great Britain in the War of 1812.
1815	Augustus Porter buys Goat Island and makes it a nature preserve.
1830s	The Welland Ship Canal is built.

1855	The first railway suspension bridge on the Niagara is opened.
1859	Jean Francois Gravelet (Charles Blondin) walks a tight rope across the Niagara Falls from the American side to the Canadian side on June 30.
1893	William T. Love announces his plan to build a manufacturing city with a long canal in Niagara Falls, New York.
1896	The first large-scale hydroelectric facility, Edward Dean Adams Power Plant, starts generating power.
1901	Annie Edson Taylor is the first person to go over the Niagara Falls on October 24.
1922	Sir Adam Beck builds the Niagara Generating Station Number One outside Queenston, Canada.
1956	The Edward Dean Adams Power Plant is destroyed on June 7.
1980	President Jimmy Carter gives the state of New York $15 million to help the former residents of Love Canal.
1990	The Niagara Escarpment is named a World Biosphere Reserve.
1996	The Environmental Protection Agency and the Justice Department announce that some parts of the Love Canal community are safe for people.

Glossary

canal lock—a part of a canal that serves as a water elevator to move ships up and down to the next section of the canal

cataract—a large waterfall, or series of waterfalls

crestline—the line that defines the shape of a waterfall

erosion—the wearing away of soil

fossil—the remains of an organism from a past geological age that is imprinted on a rock surface

friar—a member of a Roman Catholic monastic order

generator—a machine that converts energy into electrical energy

gorge—a narrow passage with steep rocky sides

hydroelectricity—the means of creating electricity by forcing rapidly running water through generators

kilowatt—a unit of electrical power

liberal—a political belief that society can be bettered through tolerance and reform.

phosphorus—a white-yellow substance that glows in the dark

portage—an overland route that connects two bodies of water or bypasses strong rapids or a waterfall

rapids—the section of a river where the current is particularly strong because the river bed has narrowed and dropped. Rapids create turbulent water

strait—a narrow channel that connects two bodies of water

suspension bridge—a bridge that hangs from cables that are secured at either end of the roadway. Often towers are placed along the roadway to support the bridge

topography—the geographic shape of a particular region

To Find Out More

Books

Berton, Pierre. *Niagara: A History of the Falls*. Toronto: McClelland & Stewart Inc., 1992.

Fisher, Leonard Everett. *Niagara Falls: Nature's Wonder*. New York: Holiday House, 1996.

Granfield, Linda. *All About Niagara Falls*. New York: Morrow Junior Books, 1996.

Hakim, Joy. *From Colonies to Country*. New York: Oxford University Press, 1993.

Heinrichs, Ann. *New York*. Danbury, CT: Children's Press, 1999.

Stowe, Harriet Beecher. *Uncle Tom's Cabin*. New York: Bantam Classic, 1983.

Organizations and Online Sites

New York History Net
http://www.nyhistory.com
This website offers many links and resources for students and teachers to find out more about the history of New York State as well as materials filled with fun facts just for kids.

New York Power Authority
http://www.nypa.gov/html/niagara.html
Read about how the New York Power Authority harnesses the Niagara to create power.

New York State Historical Maps
http://www.sunysb.edu/libmap/nymaps.htm
See how New York State changed through time by visiting the University of New York at Stony Brook's map collection online.

Niagara Parks Commission
http://www.niagaraafalls.org
Learn more about historical sites found on the Canadian side of the river from this website.

Old Fort Niagara Association
P.O. Box 169
Youngstown, NY 14174-0169
http://www.oldfortniagara.org
This organization is dedicated to preserving Fort Niagara. You can take a virtual tour of the fort on its website and learn about its history.

World Network of Biosphere Reserves
http://www.unesco.org/mab/wnbr.htm
Created by the United Nations Educational, Scientific and Cultural Organization, this website provides information on biosphere reserves, such as the Niagara Escarpment, and how they are working to protect these special environments.

A Note on Sources

When I research a book, I start at the library. Encyclopedias, magazines, books, and Internet sites are wonderful sources for information. Each fact I learn sets me off on the trail for more facts, more interesting details. When I started my research on the Niagara, I was lucky enough to begin by spending a bright summer day driving from the river's mouth at Lake Ontario to its source at Lake Erie.

Stopping wherever I wanted, I explored the Canadian side of the river. I walked through Niagara-on-the-Lake and had lunch at the MacFarland House, the only remaining pre-1812 house in the region. (The others were all destroyed during the War of 1812.) I stood on the bluffs overlooking the Niagara Gorge and watched as the river's blue green current swirled below me. I stood spellbound at the Falls and saw the sun set over Lake Erie.

I took notes, read every historical plaque I came across, and bought books I thought might help me later. *Niagara's Freedom Trail: A Guide to African-Canadian History of the Niagara Peninsula* by the Region Niagara Tourist Council was particularly helpful. So was Albert Tiplin's *Our Romantic Niagara: A Geological History of the River and the Falls.*

It is rare when any of us can do such hands-on research. So, whenever you go to a museum, visit city hall, tour a factory or a hydroelectric plant, or even walk through a historical park, remember the experience. Take pictures, take notes, check out all the available books, pamphlets, and maps. If you can, buy some. Add them to your library. You never know when the experience of that day might come in handy and trigger a book of your own.

—Melissa Whitcraft

Index

Numbers in *italics* indicate illustrations.

About the Author

Melissa Whitcraft lives in Montclair, New Jersey, with her husband, their two sons, and their dog. She has a Master of Art degree in Theatre. In addition to plays and poetry, she has published *Tales From One Street Over*, a chapter book for early elementary-grade readers. Her biography, *Francis Scott Key, a Gentleman of Maryland*, was published as a Franklin Watts First Book. Ms. Whitcraft has also written *The Tigris and Euphrates Rivers* and *The Hudson River* for the Watts Library series. Whenever possible, Ms. Whitcraft travels on rivers.